Congressional
Research
Service

Reform of U.S. International Taxation: Alternatives

Jane G. Gravelle
Senior Specialist in Economic Policy

December 27, 2012

Congressional Research Service

7-5700

www.crs.gov

RL34115

CRS Report for Congress
Prepared for Members and Committees of Congress

Summary

A striking feature of the modern U.S. economy is its growing openness—its increased integration with the rest of the world. The attention of tax policymakers has recently been focused on the growing participation of U.S. firms in the international economy and the increased pressure that engagement places on the U.S. system for taxing overseas business. Is the current U.S. tax system for taxing U.S. international business the appropriate one for the modern era of globalized business operations, or should its basic structure be reformed?

The current U.S. system for taxing international business is a hybrid. In part the system is based on a residence principle, applying U.S. taxes on a worldwide basis to U.S. firms while granting foreign tax credits to alleviate double taxation. The system, however, also permits U.S. firms to defer foreign-source income indefinitely—a feature that approaches a territorial tax jurisdiction. In keeping with its mixed structure, the system produces a patchwork of economic effects that depend the location of foreign investment and the circumstances of the firm. Broadly, the system poses a tax incentive to invest in countries with low-tax rates of their own and a disincentive to invest in high-tax countries. In theory, U.S. investment should be skewed towards low-tax countries and away from high-tax locations.

Evaluations of the current tax system vary, and so do prescriptions for reform. According to traditional economic analysis, world economic welfare is maximized by a system that applies the same tax burden to prospective (marginal) foreign and domestic investment so that taxes do not distort investment decisions. Such a system possesses "capital export neutrality," and could be accomplished by worldwide taxation applied to all foreign operations along with an unlimited foreign tax credit. In contrast, a system that maximizes national welfare—a system possessing "national neutrality"—would impose a higher tax burden on foreign investment, thus permitting an overall disincentive for foreign investment. Such a system would impose worldwide taxation, but would permit only a deduction, and not a credit, for foreign taxes.

A tax system based on territorial taxation would exempt overseas business investment from U.S. tax. In recent years, several proponents of territorial taxation have argued that changes in the world economy have rendered traditional prescriptions for international taxation obsolete, and instead prescribe territorial taxation as a means of maximizing both world and national economic welfare. For such a system to be neutral, however, capital would have to be completely immobile across locations. A case might be made that such a system is superior to the current hybrid system, but it is not clear that it is superior to other reforms, including not only a movement toward worldwide taxation by ending deferral, but also restricting deductions for costs associated with deferred income or restricting deferral and foreign tax credits for tax havens.

Contents

Tables

Contacts

T he increasingly global scope of U.S. business has a variety of dimensions. In trade, the overall level of exports plus imports has risen steadily and substantially in recent decades, increasing from 16% of U.S. gross domestic product (GDP) in 1976 to a 25% of GDP in 2009. Cross-border investment is growing even more dramatically. In 1976, the ratio of U.S. private assets to GDP was 0.20; by year end 2009 the ratio was 1.01.[1]

The bulk of the increase in "outbound" investment has been portfolio investment—investment in financial assets such as stocks and bonds without the active conduct of overseas business operations. But foreign direct investment by U.S. firms—actual foreign production by U.S.-owned companies—has increased too, rising from a ratio of 0.12 to 0.28 of GDP between 1976 and 2009. It is the taxation of U.S. business operations that has been the recent focus of policymakers, and that has raised the question of basic tax reform in the international sector: is the current U.S. tax system for taxing U.S. international business appropriate in this age of globalized business operations, or is reform needed?[2] Moreover, along with the increasing scope of international investment activities, there is an increasing opportunity for tax shelters that take advantage of low-tax foreign jurisdictions. How might revisions in the tax system exacerbate or address these tax shelter issues?

The current U.S. system is a "hybrid" construct, embodying a mix of opposing jurisdictional principles. Not surprisingly, the mixed system—in conjunction with foreign host-country taxes—poses a patchwork of incentive effects for U.S. firms and their global operations, in some cases taxing foreign operations favorably and posing an incentive to invest abroad, and in other cases imposing high tax burdens and posing a disincentive to overseas investment. In some cases, the system presents a rough tax neutrality towards overseas investment. It is perhaps the hybrid nature of the system that has led to calls for reform. Prescriptions for a "good" tax system vary, and the hybrid system satisfies none of them fully.

The report describes and assesses the principal prescriptions that have been offered for broad reform of the international system. The report begins with an overview of current law and of possible revisions. It then sets the framework for considering economic efficiency as well as tax shelter activities. Finally, it reviews alternative approaches to revision in light of those issues.

---

[1] Data on trade, U.S. assets abroad, and foreign assets in the United States are from the website of the U.S. Department of Commerce, Bureau of Economic Analysis, at http://www.bea.gov. The fixed assets data were adjusted to include estimated stocks of inventory and intangible capital.

[2] Interest in international reform comes from a variety of sources. For example, the President's executive order (E.O. 13369) establishing his advisory panel on tax reform cited international competitiveness concerns as one principal reason for considering tax reform; the panel's final report included a fundamental change in the structure of the U.S. international system as part of one of its reform options. See President's Advisory Panel on Federal Tax Reform, *Simple, Fair, and Pro-Growth: Proposals to Fix America's Tax System* (Washington, November 2005). In Congress, in June 2006, the House Ways and Means Committee's Subcommittee on Select Revenue Measures held a hearing on international tax reform. The topic is also receiving attention in the academic and professional world: the *National Tax Journal* published a four-article forum on international tax reform in its December 2001 issue.

The Current System and Possible Revisions

The System's Structure

There are two alternative, conceptually "pure," principles on which countries base their tax in the international setting: residence and territory. Under a residence system, a country taxes its own residents (or domestically chartered "resident" corporations) on their worldwide income, regardless of its geographic source. Under a territorial or source-based system, a country taxes only income that is earned within its own borders.

In practice, no country uses a pure residence-based tax; historically, virtually all countries tax income foreign investors earn within their borders (although they may grant tax holidays in some cases as an inducement to investment). Some countries, however, do have an exclusively territorial or source-based tax.[3] The United States uses a system that taxes both income of foreign firms earned within its borders as well as the worldwide income of its U.S.-chartered firms.

Despite these nominal "residence" features, however, U.S. taxes do not apply to the foreign income of U.S.-owned corporations chartered abroad. As a result, a U.S. firm can indefinitely defer U.S. tax on its foreign income if it conducts its foreign operations through a foreign-chartered subsidiary corporation; U.S. taxes do not apply as long as the foreign subsidiary's income is reinvested overseas. With some exceptions, U.S. taxes apply only when the income is remitted to the U.S.-resident parent as dividends or other intra-firm payments such as interest and royalties. The deferral feature reduces the effective U.S. tax burden on foreign income and imparts an element of territoriality to the system; it also results in a dichotomous structure for taxing overseas business income: deferral in the case of foreign-subsidiary income and current taxation in the case of branches of U.S. chartered corporations. The bulk of active business investment by U.S. firms is through foreign-chartered subsidiaries.[4]

Along with deferral, another basic feature of the U.S. system is the foreign tax credit. While the United States taxes worldwide income on either a current or deferred basis, it also allows credits for foreign taxes paid on a dollar-for-dollar basis against U.S. taxes otherwise owed.[5] This treatment avoids the double-taxation that would otherwise apply and concedes the first right of taxation to the country of source. In effect, the United States gives the foreign host country the

---

[3] President Bush's Advisory Panel on Tax Reform published a list of countries that use a territorial system either by statute or treaty. The territorial countries are: Australia, Austria, Belgium, Canada, Denmark, Finland, France, Germany, Greece, Hungary, Iceland, Italy, Luxembourg, Netherlands, Norway, Portugal, Slovak Republic, Spain, Sweden, Switzerland, and Turkey. The following countries tax foreign-source income at some point and rely on foreign tax credits to relieve double taxation: Czech Republic, Iceland, Japan, Korea, Mexico, New Zealand, Poland, the United Kingdom, and the United States. President's Advisory Panel on Federal Tax Reform, *Simple, Fair, and Pro-Growth: Proposals to Fix America's Tax System* (Washington, November 2005), p. 243. Japan and the United Kingdom, however, have recently moved to a territorial system.

[4] According to IRS data for 2008, before-tax earnings and profits of foreign subsidiaries was $661 billion while branch gross income was $178 billion. The data are posted on the IRS website at http://www.irs.gov/uac/SOI-Tax-Stats—International-Business-Tax-Statistics.

[5] U.S. parent firms are permitted to claim foreign tax credits for foreign taxes paid by their foreign-chartered subsidiaries. Such "indirect" credits can be claimed by the parent when the foreign-source income is remitted as dividends.

---

first opportunity to tax the income, and collects only what tax is left (up to its own rate) after the foreign host country collects its share.

When the foreign tax is higher than the U.S. tax, the credit is limited to the U.S. tax that would be due on the foreign income. The purpose of the limit is to protect the U.S. domestic tax base: without it, foreign countries could impose very high taxes without discouraging inbound U.S. investment, because the cost of the higher taxes would be shifted to the U.S. treasury. With the limitation, if foreign taxes exceed the U.S. tax that would be due, the excess foreign taxes cannot be credited. Foreign tax credits that exceed this limitation are termed "excess credits." Currently foreign tax credits are allowed on what is sometimes termed an "overall" basis, so that income and tax credits from all countries are combined. This treatment allows for "cross-crediting," where credits paid in excess of U.S. tax in one country may be used to offset U.S. tax in a country where the foreign tax is lower than the U.S. tax. To prevent abuse, tax credits are divided into "baskets" which separate passive income easily shifted to low-tax countries. Currently, there are two baskets, one for active income and one for passive income. Over half of foreign-source active business income is earned by firms with overall excess credits.[6]

To address tax avoidance by shifting passive income into low-tax jurisdictions, Subpart F restricts the applicability of deferral in some situations. Subpart F provides that U.S. stockholders (e.g., parent firms) of foreign corporations are subject to current U.S. tax on certain types of subsidiary income, whether or not the income is repatriated. Only stockholders owning at least 10% of subsidiary stock and only subsidiaries that are at least 50% owned by 10% U.S. stockholders are subject to Subpart F. Countries that have territorial tax systems generally also have some type of anti-abuse provision to protect their tax base.

Tax deferral results in heightened importance for the system's rules for dividing income between related firms; the more income a firm can assign, for tax purposes, to a foreign subsidiary in a low-tax country, the lower its overall tax burden. The current system generally requires firms to set hypothetical "transfer prices," which are required to approximate the prices two firms would agree on if they conducted their transactions at arm's length. The system is complex and difficult to administer.

The foreign tax credit's limitation also places pressure on the system's rules for determining the source of income ("sourcing" rules). Because firms can only credit foreign taxes against the portion of taxable income attributable to foreign sources, taxpayers must assign both revenue and costs to either domestic or foreign sources. While the tax code contains rules for making such allocations, they are likewise complex and difficult to administer.

In sum, the United States taxes its resident corporations on their worldwide income, but permits indefinite deferral of active business income earned through foreign subsidiaries. Where U.S. taxes apply, foreign tax credits alleviate double taxation but are limited to offsetting U.S. tax on foreign income. Subpart F is designed to deny deferral to what is generally passive income.

---

[6] Jennifer Gravelle reports 62% of income in 2008 was earned by firms with excess credits in at least one basket; Presentation at National Tax Association Meetings, Providence, Rhode Island, November 2012. Similar shares were found in the past. See Rosanne Altshuler and Harry Grubert, 'Corporate Taxes in the World Economy: Reforming the Taxation of Cross-Border Income," *In Fundamental Tax Reform: Issues, Choices and Implications*, Ed. John W. Diamond and George R. Zodrow, The MIT Press, Cambridge, MA, 2008.

Possible Revisions

Because the current U.S. tax system is a mix of a worldwide system and a territorial system, the fundamental tax reform issue is whether moving toward either "pure" system—a territorial or worldwide residence-based regime—would be an improvement. Moving toward a territorial system would involve permanently exempting most foreign-source active business income. (Most territorial proposals, however, would continue taxing passive income, as under current law's Subpart F.) Moving toward a worldwide tax would eliminate the deferral benefit and might also entail further restricting cross-crediting by increasing the number of baskets for the foreign tax credit limit. Some revisions that maintain the current system but tighten the rules for deductions include proposals to disallow certain deductions of the parent company (such as interest) that reflect the share of income that is deferred.

The report defers the discussion of the precise changes fundamental reform would entail. First, however, the report explains the tools economists have developed for evaluating the various international tax systems.

Neutrality, Efficiency, and Competitiveness

The term competitiveness has often been invoked in the debate about U.S. policy in a global economy, including discussions of U.S. tax policy.[7] In economic analysis, however, it is not *countries* that are competitive, it is *companies* that are. A company generally thinks of itself as competitive if it can produce at the same cost as, or a lower cost than, other firms. But a country's firms cannot be competitive in all areas. Indeed, even if firms in a country are more productive than firms in all other countries in every respect, a country would still tend to produce those goods in which its relative advantage is greatest. The other countries need to produce goods with their resources as well. This notion is called comparative advantage, and it is an important concept in economic theory.[8]

When discussing national policy, including tax policy and its effect on the international allocation of capital, the issues are generally framed around issues of efficiency, neutrality, and optimal policies rather than notions of competitiveness. These terms can mean the same thing, or they can be slightly different. Neutrality generally refers to provisions that do not alter the allocation of investment from that which would occur without taxes. When markets are operating efficiently, a neutral tax policy will also be an efficient policy, since it will maintain the efficient allocation that would occur without taxes. Moreover, even when there are market imperfections, neutrality may still be the policy most likely to be efficient, given the difficulty in identifying and measuring market imperfections.

---

[7] For a more detailed discussion of this concept see CRS Report RS22445, *Taxes and International Competitiveness*, by Donald J. Marples. See also Jane G. Gravelle, "Does the Concept of Competitiveness Have Meaning in Formulating Corporate Tax Policy?" *Tax Law Review*, vol. 65, no. 3, 2012, p. 323-348.

[8] Comparative advantage is not a technical or unfamiliar concept; it is a common, everyday occurrence. A lawyer may be able to do his or her paralegal employee's work more efficiently, but that activity is not the best use of his or her time. A lawyer has an absolute advantage in both law practice and paralegal work, but a comparative advantage in practicing law.

Optimal policy differs from efficiency in that it usually refers to a particular agent or actor choosing a policy that maximizes his or her own welfare. A country can also choose a policy that leads to the greatest welfare for its own citizens, even if that policy distorts the allocation of capital (is not neutral) and leads to less efficient worldwide production. The optimal policy from the perspective of a country, in other words, may not be the most efficient in terms of the worldwide allocation of capital, and may not be the optimal policy from the perspective of world economic welfare.

Economists have traditionally used three concepts to evaluate tax rules that apply to outbound investment. These concepts are referred to as neutrality concepts, although, as shown below, they are not always neutral in the sense of not distorting the allocation of investment. The concepts are capital export neutrality, capital import neutrality, and national neutrality. In order to evaluate the consequences of any multinational tax reform, it is crucial to understand these concepts, whether they are valid, and what they imply for policy. The concepts were developed when virtually all foreign investment took place as direct investment of multinational companies; virtually no foreign portfolio investment (ownership of foreign stock by U.S. citizens) existed. The growth in this portfolio investment has led to a new neutrality concept, referred to as capital ownership neutrality. We address these traditional and new concepts in turn.

Understanding Capital Export Neutrality, Capital Import Neutrality, and National Neutrality

Capital export neutrality requires a country to apply the same tax rate to its firms' investments, regardless of where they are located, and is embodied in a residence-based tax system. Capital import neutrality requires the same tax on firms with different nationalities that invest in a given location and is embodied in a territorial or source-based tax. National neutrality requires that the nation's total return on investment, including both that nation's taxes and its firms' profits, is equal in each jurisdiction, foreign and domestic. This form of neutrality is obtained by taxing foreign-source income and allowing a deduction for foreign taxes.

Some of these neutrality rules may also be rules for optimization. National neutrality is often described as optimal, but that outcome is only the case with perfectly mobile capital and no retaliation by foreign countries. There is also an optimizing rule for choosing the tax rate on inbound investment, which depends on how responsive that investment inflow is to the return.

Evaluating policy, discussed subsequently, is complicated because while some countries have territorial or source-based taxes, no country imposes a pure residence-based tax. While worldwide taxation as practiced in the United States and other countries has some attributes of a residence-based tax, it is a mixture of residence- and source-based tax. Tax is imposed on foreign firms operating within the United States, a source-based attribute. On outbound investment, the application of tax to repatriated income creates some resemblance to residence tax, but the foreign tax credit limitations cause it to depart from such a tax, and deferral provisions introduce an element of a source-based tax.

Because these concepts are so frequently misunderstood, it is useful to employ a simple illustrative example to explain them with the pure tax systems that are consistent with capital export neutrality and capital import neutrality. In these simple systems, national neutrality is the same as capital export neutrality, and its nuances will be discussed in the following section where more realistic tax systems are discussed. In this instance, it may be helpful to demonstrate the difference between residence-based and source-based taxes in achieving economic neutrality.

Consider a world beginning with no taxes, and assume that capital is perfectly substitutable across countries, implying that a firm will earn the same after-tax return in each location. The return is 10%. There are three countries: a high-tax country that imposes a 50% tax rate, a low-tax country that imposes a 25% tax rate, and a zero-tax country. All investment is made through the companies' direct operations, hence, there is no substitution of capital across firms and the capital owned by each country is fixed. The high and low-tax rate countries have capital which can be used to invest in their own country, or in the other two countries. To simplify, the zero-tax country is assumed to have only labor and no capital.

Table 1 shows the return to firms in the absence of any tax and with the two tax systems in place but before investment has shifted (which would alter the pre-tax return). Residence taxation, which produces capital export neutrality, has no effect on the allocation of investment by either country's firms because each firm still earns the same return in each location. Source-based taxation, however, will result in higher returns in the zero- and, to a lesser extent, low-tax countries. As a result, capital will flow out of the high-tax country, raising its return and lowering the wages of the workers in that country and into the zero-tax country, lowering its return and raising the wages of the workers in that country. The effect on the low-tax country depends on the size of that country and its labor force relative to the rest of the world. In addition to the effects on the return to capital and wages, output is produced inefficiently, which reduces world welfare.

Table 1. Illustration of the Effects of Residence- and Source-Based Taxation

Nationality of Firm	Return by Location of Investment (%)		
	High-Tax Country	Low-Tax Country	Zero-Tax Country
No Taxes			
High-Tax Country	10%	10%	10%
Low-Tax Country	10%	10%	10%
Residence Tax			
High-Tax Country	5%	5%	5%
Low-Tax Country	7.5%	7.5%	7.5%
Source-Based (Territorial) Tax			
High-Tax Country	5%	7.5%	10%
Low-Tax Country	5%	7.5%	10%

Note: The high-tax country has a 50% tax rate, while the low-tax country has a 25% tax rate.

Table 1 can also be used to show that the residence-based system is also consistent with national neutrality, but the source-based system is not. For the high-tax country, in each location it earns 5% in tax revenue and 5% in profits (for a total of 10%). Thus the total return to the nation is equated in each jurisdiction. The same is true of the low-tax country, although the total return is split into 2.5% taxes and 7.5% profits. The source-based system does not meet that standard. Even before investment shifts, the high-tax country, while earning 10% domestically and in the zero tax haven country, is earning only 7.5% in the low-tax country, since that country's government is collecting the tax. The same is true of the low-tax country with respect to investment taxed by the high-tax country.

National neutrality departs from capital export neutrality in the more complex, real world circumstances. It, in fact, requires that foreign-source income be taxed, and that any taxes imposed by the country of location be deducted (rather than the current rule of some countries, including the United States, that allow taxes to be credited). If foreign countries impose taxes, national neutrality does not lead to worldwide neutrality, since foreign investment is discouraged in countries that impose taxes.

National neutrality is really about optimal policy, which maximizes the welfare of the country's residents. It is an optimal policy if all capital is perfectly mobile; if not, it is actually optimal for a country to impose even more tax on outbound investment than is suggested by the neutrality standard.

In sum, according to these longstanding measures of neutrality and efficiency, capital export neutrality is appropriate for maximizing world output, national neutrality is appropriate for maximizing a nation's welfare, and capital import "neutrality" is not neutral at all.

Capital Ownership Neutrality

A new concept of neutrality has appeared in recent years. The term capital ownership neutrality (CON) is closely associated with Desai and Hines, professors, respectively, of business at Harvard and economics at the University of Michigan.[9] The term itself, however, appears to have been coined by Michael Devereaux,[10] a British economist. The underlying justification for the new standard's development, the growth of portfolio investment, was also discussed independently about the same time in a paper by Frisch.[11] Essentially, capital ownership neutrality is the same as capital import neutrality in that, under certain very restrictive assumptions, it is achieved by source-based taxation, and some of the earlier discussions viewed it as a resurrection of capital import neutrality.[12]

The issue of ownership neutrality developed because international investment markets changed. At the time the previous notions of neutral international tax systems were first developed— generally, the early 1960s—virtually all U.S. investment abroad was carried out through foreign direct investment by U.S. firms.[13] U.S. portfolio investors held almost no stock in foreign firms. Until the mid-1980s, the share of foreign stocks in U.S. residents' stock portfolios was less than

---

[9] Mihir Desai and James Hines, Evaluating International Tax Reform, *National Tax Journal*, vol. 56, September 2003.

[10] Michael P. Devereux, "Capital Export Neutrality, Capital Import Neutrality, Capital Ownership Neutrality, and All That," Unpublished Paper, June 11, 1990.

[11] Daniel J. Frisch, "The Economics of International Tax Policy: Some Old and New Approaches," *Tax Notes*, April 30, 1990.

[12] Frisch, in "The Economics of International Tax Policy: Some Old and New Approaches," states, "In short, a major element of the CIN view would seem to possess a grain of truth," (p. 590) referring to the capital import neutrality framework. Devereux, in "Capital Export Neutrality, Capital Import Neutrality, Capital Ownership Neutrality, and All That," indicated that he originally attempted to redefine capital import neutrality to cover the capital ownership neutrality concept.

[13] The concepts were first developed by Peggy Musgrave. See, for example, her *United States Taxation of Foreign Investment Income: Issues and Arguments* (Cambridge MA: Harvard Law School, 1969), pp. 108-121.

1%. Thus, it was reasonable to assume, as in the discussion above, that there was no substitution across the nationality of firms, but rather only across locations—that is, U.S. investors could not substitute investment abroad through foreign firms for investment in U.S. firms with foreign operations. Over time, however, the share of foreign stock owned by U.S. investors increased, and by the end of 2006, it was 22% of corporate equity owned by U.S. investors.[14] This increase did not occur smoothly: it increased in the latter part of the mid-1980s to about 6%, leveled out for a number of years, then again rose around 1993 and 1994 to about 11%, where it stayed until around 2001, and then rose again.

A closer look at the CON concept indicates that, to make the argument that capital ownership neutrality (and therefore source-based taxation) should be the guiding principle for an efficient and neutral tax system, three requirements are needed. First, firms are assumed not to substitute operations in one location for those in another—capital is completely immobile across locations. Second, firms must differ in their productivity—that is, some firms are more efficient than others—and there must be substitution across portfolios that results in firms being shut out of lines-of-business that they could run more efficiently. Third, there must be no mechanisms available to obtain the benefits of productive efficiency—short of owning the productive capital assets. For example, relatively inefficient firms cannot rent efficient technologies or hire efficient managers away from efficient firms.

If only the first requirement is met (immobility across locations), any system of taxing investment abroad would be neutral because the particular distortion—allocation of investment across locations—is simply assumed away. It doesn't matter if overseas operations are taxed higher or lower than domestic investment, because investment has no reason to move. Residence taxation would be efficient as well as source-based taxation, because the national affiliation of firms would not matter to productivity (although residence taxation would not be optimal for the high-tax country which would have no revenues).[15]

If the two remaining assumptions also apply—productivity differs and no mechanisms exist to boost efficiency—it can be shown that residence-based taxation is inefficient while source-based taxation produces efficiency. For example, returning to **Table 1**, suppose some firms in each country are particularly productive and can earn 12% before tax rather than 10%. With residence-based taxation, the after-tax return of the high-tax country's productive firms, which would yield an after-tax return of 6%, would not be enough for these firms to operate and, if the only way to realize the higher return is to own the capital, the higher pre-tax yields of these more efficient firms would not be realized. With source-based taxation, the efficient firms in each country would operate and displace the less efficient ones.

In the more realistic tax systems where countries also tax capital income in their own location, the high-tax country's especially productive firms would still operate in their own country. That is, by taxing income within its borders, a high-tax country that is attempting to practice capital export neutrality with a worldwide tax still faces neutral ground in its home country. Thus, any distortion

---

[14] Calculated by reducing U.S. corporate equity issues by foreign stock holdings in the United States determining U.S. holdings of foreign stocks as a share. Data on corporate equities can be found in the Board of Governors of the Federal Reserve Flow of Funds Accounts, Table L213, which can be found at http://www.federalreserve.gov/releases/Z1/Current/. Historical series can also be found in the National Income and Product Accounts at http://www.bea.gov/national/nipaweb/Ni_FedBeaSna/TableView.asp?SelectedTable=5&FirstYear=1998&LastYear=2005&Freq=Year.

[15] This optimality issue has also been addressed with the notion of National Ownership Neutrality, which indicates that it is both efficient and optimal to have source-based taxation.

---

arising in practice from the current system would involve foreign firms and the solution of exempting foreign-source income from tax is the solution consistent with capital ownership neutrality.

Consider each of the restrictions in turn. The first is the assumption that capital is immobile across locations; as noted above, there is considerable evidence that it is not and, indeed, that it is quite elastic. So at best, it would be a question of picking which type of distortion is worse. As long as capital is mobile across jurisdictions, "capital ownership neutrality" is not neutral. At most, the model shows that there is no way to achieve neutrality and that one is in a second-best world.

The second restriction requires a high, perhaps perfect, degree of substitution in portfolios of different types of stocks that would lead to the exclusion of stock of high-tax countries. There is considerable evidence to suggest that such perfect substitution is not the case. It has long been known that there is a significant home bias in the holding of both portfolio and direct assets. Despite global securities markets, American residents continue to hold 80% of their stock portfolios in stock of U.S. firms. If portfolio investment were perfectly substitutable, the U.S. share would be expected to be closer to the share of total assets. The U.S. accounts for about a third of total fixed investment of the OECD countries.[16]

The fact that the portfolio share has grown does not in itself provide evidence of a significant elasticity; rather, it may reflect a variety of technical and institutional changes that make holding foreign stocks more feasible. Moreover, the portfolio shares are consistent with the notion that the holdings that do exist are not so much due to tax differences but to a general desire to diversify assets across countries to reduce cyclical risk. Two-thirds of investment is in other countries with similar tax rates. At the end of 2005, the two largest shares were for the U.K. (16%) and Japan (15%). While the U.K., with a 30% corporate rate, has a lower statutory rate than the U.S. (39% including state taxes), Japan has a rate of 41%. The next two largest claimants with 7% and 6% have rates of 35% and 35%.[17] There are significant shares in two tax havens, Bermuda (5%) and the Cayman Islands (3%). According to the Department of Treasury, however, the Bermuda investments are largely former U.S. firms that have moved their location to avoid U.S. tax (a phenomenon called inversion, which was subsequently addressed with legislative restrictions), and the Cayman Islands investments are in offshore financial centers (again likely a tax avoidance issue rather than direct production issue).[18]

An imperfect portfolio substitution elasticity also suggests that the phenomenon of eliminating efficient firms is less likely to happen. Firms that are especially productive and efficient will earn higher returns than other firms in similar circumstances of nationality and location, and they would be expected to be retained in both domestic and foreign investors' portfolios. Any firms whose size is contracted by portfolio shifts due to tax rates are more likely to be the marginal firms that have a normal level of productivity.

---

[16] Congressional Budget Office, *Corporate Tax Rates: International Comparisons,* November, 2005.

[17] Data are from tax rates cited in Congressional Budget Office. *Corporate Tax Rates: International Comparisons, November, 2005,* and portfolio share data are from U.S. Department of Treasury *Report on U.S. Portfolio Holdings of Foreign Securities.*

[18] U.S. Department of Treasury, *Report on U.S. Portfolio Holdings of Foreign Securities.*

Finally, this model assumes that there are no other ways to enjoy the additional productivity of more efficient firms. In effect, the model begins with the assumption of productive advantages without defining in formal terms—so that the effects can be modeled—the source of the productivity.

For example, if the greater productivity of the firm is due to the employment of managers with greater skills, then that productivity arises at a cost, and these management skills embodied in the individuals resident in a given country should be free to move to their highest use, and allocated efficiently. Since they add a surplus value, they would not be driven out of the market, and worldwide efficiency requires a capital export neutrality approach to labor resources as well as capital.

If the asset is uniquely tied to the firm—such as a value through a trademark, intangible R&D, or even a management set-up—the model does not allow for the fact that ownership of the productive assets and ownership of the intangible asset can, in most cases, be separated. Trademarks and patents can be franchised and sold. Or, if the intangible cannot be separately sold (for example, if the R&D could be easily copied and thus is not patented but kept secret), there are ways for the firm to operate without ownership of the capital assets, such as factories, machinery, and equipment, that give rise to normal products. These assets could be leased by the firm with the intangible asset. Moreover, if the asset is not closely tied to management, the firm could arrange for contract manufacturing, a technique commonly used to shift profits. These techniques may be less than perfect if there are principal-agent costs,[19] but this effect is of questionable importance.

In light of the many ways in which the efficiency costs of capital ownership non-neutrality are unlikely to be significant compared to location distortions, it seems questionable to use meeting this standard of neutrality to evaluate tax reform changes and questionable to see source-based taxation as an efficient international tax regime.

Assessing the Existing Tax System

The above examples illustrate the various traditional concepts of neutrality and how they are embodied in basic tax structures. However, as described at the report's outset, the U.S. tax system is a hybrid—neither a pure territorial or residence-based system. Accordingly, it presents a patchwork of incentive effects, sometimes posing an incentive to invest abroad and, in other situations, presenting either a disincentive or tax neutrality. We look in this section at the existing system's principal incentive effects.

First, in some cases the U.S. system resembles residence-based taxation—it taxes foreign branch income on a current basis while allowing a foreign tax credit. Even where current taxation applies, however, the U.S. system departs from pure residence taxation by placing a limit on its foreign tax credit. If pure residence-based means taxing income of residents at the same rate, regardless of where it is earned, an unlimited foreign tax credit would be required. Under such a credit, when the foreign tax is lower than the home country tax, the home country would collect a

---

[19] Principal-agent costs occur when the objectives of the two parties are not identical. For example, the contract manufacturer (the agent) may want to increase the scale of the operation rather than maximizing profits for the firm authorizing the manufacturing (the principal).

residual, equating the total tax imposed to that on its domestic investment. When the foreign country's tax is higher, the home country would have to refund the excess so that, again, the tax on the foreign investment would be the same as the tax on domestic investment. In practice, however, an unlimited foreign tax credit is not feasible because of its potential threat to the home country tax base (here, that of the United States). Without a limit, countries host to foreign investment could simply raise their taxes on inbound investment without limit and without fear of driving foreign investors away. The foreign investors could simply credit their high foreign taxes against their home-country tax bill. The U.S. thus limits its foreign tax credit to offsetting U.S. taxes on foreign (and not domestic) income.

The incentive effects of a worldwide system with a limited credit depend on exactly how the credit is limited. If the limit applies separately for each country (a "per-country" limit), the system would achieve neutrality on outbound investment with respect to low tax-rate countries, but not high tax-rate countries. If taxes can be averaged across countries—that is, if a firm calculates a single limit aggregated across countries, the neutrality consequences are less clear. In that case, the excess credits from the investment in a high-tax country can be used to offset tax due on investments in the low-tax country (can be "cross credited"). For example, assume profits were $100 in a high-tax location with a 50% rate and $100 in the no-tax location, with the home country tax rate 25%. With no cross crediting, a firm from the 25% tax rate country uses the foreign tax of $50 to wipe out the home country tax of $25, with only the tax of $50 applying, while the firm would pay a home country tax of $25 on the income earned in the zero tax jurisdiction. The total tax is $75. With cross crediting, the total foreign-source income is $200, the total foreign tax paid is $50 (in the high-tax country, on $100 of profit), and the total home-country tax due is also $50 (25% of $200 of income in both countries). All foreign tax is credited and the total tax is $50.

Cross crediting, as allowed in the U.S. tax system, can therefore reduce the disincentive to invest in high-tax countries if the firm already has investment in the zero tax country, because the excess credits have a value. Similarly, it can increase the incentive to invest in the zero tax country if the country already has investment in the high-tax country, since excess credits can effectively remove any residual tax in the zero tax country. In either case, foreign investment is encouraged relative to domestic investment. In practice, the U.S. tax system permits extensive cross crediting; it does not require a per-country limitation, although it does require firms to calculate separate limits for passive and active business income.

Second, the U.S. tax system departs from residence-based taxation in its use of deferral. As described above, U.S. taxes generally do not apply to the foreign business income of foreign-chartered subsidiaries. This feature of the tax system introduces elements of a territorial or source-based taxation into the system, and also introduces a distortion in firms' decisions of whether to return profits to the United States or reinvest them abroad. Moreover the interaction of deferral with cross crediting provides some scope for firms to choose the times and places of repatriation to minimize tax liability. In general, the availability of deferral—like the territorial taxation it at least approaches—poses an incentive for U.S. firms to invest in low-tax countries. Also, once capital has been invested abroad, the provision encourages firms to retain their earnings overseas rather than returning them to the United States.

This mixture of treatments also provides methods for avoiding tax apart from the direct effects on investment allocation. Deferral provides an incentive to artificially shift profits to low-tax jurisdictions. Since firms can choose between branch operations and investment via foreign-chartered subsidiaries, they can use a branch form when operations are starting up and typically lose money to allow losses to be deducted from the U.S. worldwide income tax, and then shift to a subsidiary form when the operation becomes profitable.

In sum, the current system poses a patchwork of incentive effects that is in keeping with its hybrid nature. Where current taxation applies—for example, to branch income—there is a disincentive to invest in high-tax countries, and either an incentive or neutrality towards investment in low-tax countries, depending on whether the investing firm can use cross-crediting of foreign taxes. Where deferral is available, the system poses an incentive to invest in low-tax countries. The system also provides mechanisms for artificially sheltering income from tax.

Territorial Taxation: The Dividend Exemption Proposal

The preceding sections showed why the theoretical argument that territorial taxation is optimal is difficult to defend. Some have argued, however, that while territorial taxation may not be the most efficient system in a perfect world, it is nonetheless superior to the hybrid, patchwork system that is the current U.S. system—a "second best" argument. A territorial tax was recently proposed by the National Commission on Fiscal Responsibility and Reform, although the specific details were not provided.[20] To best understand this argument for territorial taxation, it is helpful to examine the specific version proposed in a 2001 American Enterprise Institute monograph by economists Harry Grubert and John Mutti. A similar plan was set forth in 2005 by President Bush's advisory commission on tax reform.[21] While the Grubert-Mutti proposal had been the focus of attention for many years, more recent proposals, described subsequently, are quite different.

Grubert and Mutti described their proposal as a "dividend exemption" system, thus focusing on the chief modification their plan would make to the current regime: it would exempt from U.S. taxes dividends repatriated to U.S. parents from foreign subsidiary corporations, thus moving from current law's deferral for foreign income to a permanent exemption. More generally, an exemption system can be viewed as a territorial tax system whose application is restricted to active business investment abroad, but that continues to tax portfolio investment of firms (such as interest, royalties, and similar income) on a current basis.

Several additional features of the plan are important to the advantages it might have over the current system. First, the plan would not permit foreign tax credits to be claimed for foreign taxes paid with respect to repatriated earnings. The repatriations, after all, would be exempt from U.S. tax, thus obviating the need for relief from double taxation. Second, deductions allocable to tax-exempt foreign-source income would be disallowed. Here, the reasoning is that the purpose of deductions is to remove items of cost from the tax base; since overseas income would no longer be in the U.S. tax base, removal of associated costs would not be necessary. Importantly, this

---

[20] National Commission on Fiscal Responsibility and Reform, The Moment of Truth., Washington, D.C., The White House, December 2010.

[21] Harry Grubert and John Mutti, *Taxing International Business Income: Dividend Exemption versus the Current System* (Washington: American Enterprise Institute, 2001), 67 pp; President's Advisory Panel on Tax Reform, *Simple, Fair, and Pro-Growth: Proposals to Fix America's Tax System* (Washington, 1985), pp. 239-244.

---

would mean that a portion of debt incurred by a U.S. parent corporation would not be deductible—the portion assumed to be used in financing tax-exempt foreign subsidiaries.

As described in the preceding sections, the capital import neutrality and capital ownership neutrality standards both recommend adoption of territorial taxation, but traditional economic theory is skeptical of the theoretical justification of the two standards. Grubert and Mutti argue, however, that even if CIN and CON are rejected on theoretical grounds, an exemption system is superior to the current hybrid system in terms of several important factors: efficiency, simplicity, and the raising of tax revenue.

First, efficiency: Grubert and Mutti argue that current law's application of tax to repatriated foreign earnings encourages wasteful and inefficient behavior on the part of corporations in devising methods of repatriating foreign earnings without paying U.S. tax. Under an exemption system, such wasteful planning would be unnecessary. Also, since foreign tax credits would no longer be applicable, cross-crediting of excess foreign tax credits would no longer shield investment in low-tax foreign locations from U.S. tax, and the artificial diversion of technology-exploiting investment to low-tax locations would no longer occur.[22]

Nevertheless, elimination of these sources of inefficiency alone would not be sufficient to make an exemption system less wasteful than current law. If elimination of tax on repatriations were the only feature of an exemption system, the system would likely increase inefficiency by encouraging added investment in low-tax countries. Rather, the crucial element to an exemption system's purported superiority is its elimination of interest deductions for overseas investment. The inclusion of this provision would actually result in an increase in the average tax burden for overseas investment, thus generating an efficiency gain from an improved allocation of investment away from low-tax overseas locations and into the domestic economy.[23]

An exemption system may also increase tax revenue. The Grubert and Mutti analysis concludes that the system would generate $7.7 billion annually in added U.S. revenue.[24] (Their estimate is based on 1994 data, so it would likely be larger in the current economy.) More recently, the Joint Committee on Taxation has estimated the revenue gain at about $6 billion per year.[25] As with the efficiency gains, however, the increase in tax revenues is crucially dependent on denial of deductions for costs allocated to tax-exempt foreign income. Without the new restrictions, an exemption system would likely reduce tax revenue. The Joint Committee on Taxation has estimated that current law's deferral reduces revenues by approximately $6 billion.[26] By the same

---

[22] Ibid., p. 11. Note, however, that cross-crediting also reduces current law's inefficient disincentive to invest in high-tax countries on the part of firms without excess credits, a feature not considered by the Grubert/Mutti analysis. Because income earned by firms with a deficit of credits outweighs that of firms with excess credits, it is plausible that an exemption system's loss of this easing of inefficiency would outweigh the gains from reduced investment in low-tax countries.

[23] Writing more recently, Grubert and his co-author Rosanne Altshuler note that if an exemption system is actively considered by policymakers, its adoption with its full panoply of deduction restrictions intact would be problematic. Rosanne Altshuler and Harry Grubert, *Corporate Taxes in the World Economy: Reforming the Taxation of Cross-Border Income*, unpublished paper presented at the James A. Baker II Inst. for Public Policy conference on tax reform, April 27-28, 2006, p. 4.

[24] Harry Grubert and John Mutti, *Taxing International Business Income*, p. 38.

[25] Report in U.S. Congressional Budget Office, *Budget Options* (Washington, February 2007), p. 319.

[26] Joint Committee on Taxation, *Estimates of Federal Tax Expenditures 2006-2010*, JCS-2-06, April 25, 2006.

---

token, an exemption system would lose tax revenue compared to the current system if the current system were to deny deductions to deferred income.

In the area of simplicity, proponents of an exemption system emphasize its reduction in the need for tax planning. It should be noted, however, that tax complexity—and its accompanying difficulties for tax administration—exist when entities or activities are taxed according to different rules. Under an exemption system, foreign subsidiary corporations would be tax exempt as under current law, and since the exemption would be permanent rather than temporary, its import for firms' tax planners would be magnified. Accordingly, the tax system's transfer pricing rules for allocating income among U.S. parent firms and their foreign subsidiaries would become more important; more pressure would apply to rules that are inherently difficult to enforce. The same would be true for the distinction between active and passive income, since active income would be permanently exempt and passive-investment income would be taxed on a current basis. Firms would have an even greater incentive to move from branch to subsidiary operations for start-up firms.

In a recent article critical of territorial tax proposals, Kleinbard pointed out analyses by Grubert and others that emphasized the growth in the importance of royalties as a share of repatriated earnings for multinationals, suggesting that the exploitation of intangible assets by multinationals in foreign locations is increasing. However, where the Grubert and Mutti analysis sees this as an important reason to adopt an exemption system—cross-crediting of foreign taxes would no longer pose an incentive to low-tax investment under an exemption system—Kleinbard sees it as a liability. The growth of intangibles, argues Kleinbard, would place enormous pressure on the administration of transfer prices.[27]

Proponents of an exemption system concede that it is not perfect, but argue that it is at least superior to the highly imperfect system now in existence. Even this defense, however, has its shortcomings: the most economically attractive aspects of the exemption proposals could, in principle, be adopted piecemeal, and its most distortionary aspects could be left behind. Specifically, more restrictive rules for deducting interest and other costs could be adopted without exempting dividend repatriations from U.S. tax. Such plans could enhance economic efficiency more than would the full-blown exemption systems.

More recent proposals, such as those proposed by the Ways and Means Committee and in a bill by Senator Enzi (S. 2091), differ in substantial ways from the Mutti-Grubert proposal. They do not include the allocation of deductions and propose, or consider, some relief for royalties. These proposals also contain anti-base erosion provisions or options for limiting profit shifting whose adoption and effectiveness is uncertain. Finally, they propose to be revenue neutral in the budget horizon but this neutrality relies on a one time taxation of existing accumulated earnings and thus would lose revenue in the long run. On the whole, therefore, these proposals would likely encourage more investment abroad. The fleshing out of a detailed territorial tax provision that might be considered legislatively has also served to highlight one of the major concerns about moving to a territorial tax: the possible increase in international profit shifting and tax avoidance.[28]

---

[27] Edward D. Kleinbard, "Throw Territorial Taxation from the Train," *Tax Notes,* February 5, 2007, pp. 552-553.

[28] For a discussion of international tax avoidance, see CRS Report R40623, *Tax Havens: International Tax Avoidance and Evasion*, by Jane G. Gravelle. For a more detailed discussion of territorial tax proposals, see CRS Report R42624, *Moving to a Territorial Income Tax: Options and Challenges*, by Jane G. Gravelle.

Even with these criticisms and even when considering the Mutti-Grubert version of the exemption, another question is this: why accept second best? The report next examines what moving towards a residence-based system would look like, in practice.

A Residence-Based System in Practice

The capital export neutrality standard recommends a system that would be based on residence— that is, a system that taxes the income of home-country firms, regardless of where it is earned. The present section looks at the shape a residence-based system would likely take.

Current law's deferral system would be repealed under a residence-based system, and U.S. taxation would apply on a current basis to the income of foreign subsidiaries, whether or not the income is repatriated. If it were not for foreign taxes, deferral's repeal would move the system to the brink of capital export neutrality (except for the portfolio investment concern): the tax burden on foreign investment would roughly equal the tax rate on domestic investment. Foreign taxes, however, complicate matters and make pure capital export neutrality difficult to achieve, in practice. The problem arises when a foreign host country's tax rate exceeds the U.S. domestic tax rate. In such cases, pure capital export neutrality would require an unlimited foreign tax credit. Foreign taxes would offset U.S. taxes on domestic as well as foreign income—only by this mechanism could the high foreign tax burden be brought into line with taxes on domestic investment. Yet, as noted in the preceding section on the existing tax system, an unlimited foreign tax credit is impractical: foreign governments could, in effect, draw on the U.S. Treasury by raising taxes on U.S. investors, *ad infinitum*.

Advocates of a residence-based system have in some cases advocated a more restrictive form of the foreign tax credit limitation that would place more limits on "cross crediting" than does current law's two-part limit. For example, at various times in the past, the United States has required firms to calculate their limitation on a country-by-country basis (a so-called "per-country" limitation), under which taxes paid to one country could not be credited against U.S. tax on income from another country.[29] The Wyden-Gregg Tax Reform Act , S. 3018, introduced in the 111th Congress would, in the context of a general corporate reform that would broaden the base and reduce the rate, eliminate deferral and institute a per country foreign tax credit limit. An alternative or additional approach to restricting cross crediting was implemented by the Tax Reform Act of 1986 (P.L. 99-514), which, instead of requiring separate limits for each country, specified a variety of different types of income for which separate limits ("baskets") were required. The American Jobs Creation Act of 2004 (AJCA; P.L. 108-357), however, reduced the number of separate limits to current law's two.[30] Note, however, that a more restrictive foreign tax credit limitation would not necessarily move a residence-based system closer to pure capital

---

[29] From 1954 to 1961, taxpayers were required to use a per-country limitation. For a synopsis of changes in limitation policy, see Thomas Horst, "The Overall vs. the Per-Country Limitation on the U.S. Foreign Tax Credit," in U.S. Department of the Treasury, Office of Tax Analysis, *1978 Compendium of Tax Research* (Washington: GPO, 1978), pp. 213-214.

[30] The purest form of a separate limitation would require a separate limitation to be calculated for each investment a firm makes. Clearly, however, such a policy would present considerable administrative difficulties.

export neutrality. As noted above, while cross crediting may pose an incentive to invest in low-tax countries, it also mitigates the disincentive to invest in high-tax countries.

Capital export neutrality requires equal tax burdens on foreign and domestic investment. There are several features of the current system that favor domestic over foreign investment, and whose modification would move the current system in the direction of capital export neutrality. The most important of these is the 9% tax deduction for domestic production enacted in 2004 by AJCA. Other tax benefits that are restricted to domestic investment are the Section 179 "expensing" allowance for machines and equipment and the research and experimentation tax credit.

As noted above, Grubert and Altshuler revisited the topic of international tax reform in 2006. In their analysis, they compared the exemption system with what they termed a "burden neutral" worldwide taxation system. In constructing this latter system, they couple elimination of deferral with a reduction in the statutory U.S. tax rate that applies to foreign earnings—thus using the added tax revenue from deferral's repeal to, in effect, "purchase" a cut in the tax rate. The goal of the exchange is to not damage what they term the "competitive position" of U.S. multinationals. As a consequence of the countervailing changes, the burden on investment in a range of low-tax countries would increase; the burden of a range of income that is repatriated under current law would fall, but the overall burden on overseas investment would be unchanged.

Grubert and Altshuler note that the overall advantage of their burden-neutral worldwide proposal over current law depends on outcomes which are, as yet, unknown: how many firms would be in an excess credit position under the plan and what the burden-neutral tax rate would be. They also caution that the plan would have another weakness: foreign countries would have an incentive to raise their tax rates in the face of current U.S. taxation because inbound U.S. investment would be less sensitive to the foreign rates.[31] They further note that their plan's reduction of tax rates at the corporate level would shift more of the overall U.S. tax burden on corporations from the corporate to the shareholder level—a virtue in the modern world where capital is increasingly mobile since shareholder-level taxes are generally imposed on a residence basis and thus achieve allocative efficiency.

President Obama's Proposals to Restrict Deferral and Cross-Crediting

It is also possible to move toward further restrictions on deferral without eliminating it entirely. One such proposal, contained in H.R. 3970, the tax reform proposal introduced by Chairman Rangel of the Ways and Means Committee, would disallow certain deductions of parent company costs (the most important being interest) that reflect the share of income that is deferred. This provisions, projected to raise revenue of $106 billion over 10 years, would make investment in low-tax countries much less attractive.[32] The revenue from this provision and other changes were to be used to lower the corporate statutory tax rate.

---

[31] Rosanne Altshuler and Harry Grubert, *Corporate Taxes in the World Economy: Reforming the Taxation of Cross-Border Income*, p. 17.

[32] The provisions of H.R. 3970 are discussed in CRS Report RL34249, *The Tax Reduction and Reform Act of 2007: An Overview*, by Jane G. Gravelle. The bill also contains a provision that repeals a planned liberalization of interest allocation rules for purposes of the foreign tax credit limit. This provision is discussed in CRS Report RL34494, *The* (continued...)

This proposal also included a foreign tax credit pooling proposal, which would allow a share of foreign tax credits equal to the share of income repatriated. This provision limits the ability of firms to repatriate income from high tax countries and use excess foreign tax credits to shield income from low tax countries from the foreign tax credit. President Obama proposed these changes, along with others, in his various budget proposals.[33] (The allocation of deductions, however, excluded research and development expenditures). The deferral provision was projected to raise $5.9 billion in FY2014 and $37.2 billion over 10 years and the foreign credit and the foreign tax credit pooling provision was projected to raise $5.5 billion in FY2013 and $60.8 billion over 10 years.

Another provision (contained in the FY2010 proposals, but not in later outlines) would eliminate "check-the-box," a provision that allows firms to elect to treat subsidiaries as separate entities or disregarded entities. These regulations permit firms to avoid current taxation on certain income that would be subject to Subpart F anti-abuse rules (such as interest on loans from a subsidiary in a low tax country to a related subsidiary in a high tax country). This provision was originally projected to raise $86 billion over 10 years.[34]

A provision in the FY2013 proposal would treat excess income from intangibles as Subpart F income and assigns them to a separate foreign tax credit basket. This provision is projected to raise $2.7 billion in FY2014, and $23.0 billion over 10 years. It may have been a substitute for "check-the-box" revisions.

The proposals also included a provision that would disallow foreign tax credits when the associated income is not received, as can occur with an arrangement termed a "reverse hybrids." This provision was adopted in 2010 (P.L. 111-226). P.L. 111-226 contained a number of provisions that were directed at perceived abuses of the foreign tax credit. Several other more limited proposals were included in the President's budget proposals.[35] In the FY2013 proposal, these international proposals are projected to raise $16.2 billion in FY2014 and $147.5 over 10 years.

The Administration also presented a framework for tax reform that mentioned five elements: the allocation of interest for deferred income (first bullet point above), a tax on excess intangibles (third bullet point), a minimum tax on foreign source income in low tax countries, disallowing a deduction for the cost of moving abroad, and providing a 20% credit for costs of moving an operation from abroad to the United States.[36]

(...continued)

Foreign Tax Credit's Interest Allocation Rules, by Jane G. Gravelle and Donald J. Marples.

[33] U.S. Department of Treasury,. General Explanations of the Administration's Fiscal Year 2013 Revenue Proposals (Green Book), Washington, DC, February, 2012. http://www.treasury.gov/resource-center/tax-policy/Documents/General-Explanations-FY2013-Tables.pdf.

[34] U.S. Department of Treasury. General Explanations of the Administration's Fiscal Year 2010 Revenue Proposals (Green Book), Washington, DC, May 2009. http://www.treasury.gov/resource-center/tax-policy/Documents/General-Explanations-FY2010.pdf.

[35] See CRS Report R40623, *Tax Havens: International Tax Avoidance and Evasion*, by Jane G. Gravelle, for a summary of these enacted and proposed revisions.

[36] *The President's Framework for Business Tax Reform: A Joint Report by the White House and the Department of the Treasury*, February 2012, http://www.treasury.gov/resource-center/tax-policy/Documents/The-Presidents-Framework-for-Business-Tax-Reform-02-22-2012.pdf.

A minimum tax on foreign source income might be a compromise between moving to a territorial system and eliminating deferral. Another form of compromise might be requiring a percentage of income to be paid out.

Tax Havens: Issues and Policy Options

The topic of "tax havens" has been a focus of recent international tax policy discussions. (This topic is treated in more detail in another CRS report.)[37] Tax havens do not fit neatly into the traditional CEN/CMN/NN evaluation framework outlined above—perhaps because the tax haven issue involves as much artificial shifting of income and investment as it does questions about how investment is actually allocated. To the extent tax havens abet the shifting of income from its true geographic source to low-tax jurisdictions (the havens themselves), they raise questions about protecting the U.S. Treasury from revenue losses. They also raise questions about tax fairness (not all taxpayers are in position to reduce their U.S. taxes by using tax havens). And to the extent tax havens reduce the tax burden on investment that truly occurs overseas, they also raise the same questions about economic efficiency and neutrality addressed by the traditional framework outlined above.

"Tax haven" is not a precisely defined term, but in most usages it refers to a country—in many cases small ones—where non-residents can save taxes by conducting various investments, transactions, and activities. Attributes that make a country a successful tax haven include low or non-existent tax rates applicable to foreigners; strict bank and financial secrecy laws; and a highly developed communications, financial, and legal infrastructure.

At the heart of the tax haven issue is the discrepancy between real economic activity and what is only apparent. Much of the economic activity that appears to occur in tax havens actually occurs elsewhere, and is only associated with particular tax haven countries because of sometimes spurious relationships between the person or firm conducting the activity and the tax-haven country. Thus, for example, much (or even most) of the income reported by U.S.-controlled subsidiaries chartered in tax havens may well have its true economic location either in some other foreign country or even in the United States itself. In several small tax haven locations, income of U.S.-controlled foreign subsidiaries are many times larger than GDP. In Bermuda and the Cayman Islands, this income was respectively, over six times and over five times.[38]

In part, U.S. firms may find tax havens useful tax-saving mechanisms because of particular aspects of the U.S. tax structure. Here, no illegal tax evasion or even transfer-price manipulation may be necessary to obtain tax savings. An example is the technique sometimes termed a corporate "inversion" reorganization, under which the overall parent of a corporate group shifts from a U.S.-chartered entity to a foreign corporation organized in an offshore tax haven. The rearrangement can potentially reduce or eliminate U.S. tax that would otherwise be due when foreign income is repatriated.[39]

---

[37] CRS Report R40623, *Tax Havens: International Tax Avoidance and Evasion*, by Jane G. Gravelle.

[38] Ibid., see Table 4.

[39] For more information, see CRS Report RL31444, *Firms That Incorporate Abroad for Tax Purposes: Corporate "Inversions" and "Expatriation"*, by Donald J. Marples.

U.S. firms can also use tax havens to shift income out of foreign countries where there are corporate income taxes to the zero-tax environment many tax havens offer. Short of outright tax evasion, techniques for shifting income include manipulation of transfer prices affixed to intrafirm sales and other transfers, and the structuring of intrafirm lending and interest charges so as to shift income out of high-tax countries to tax havens (sometimes called "earnings stripping"). Transfer price manipulation can also theoretically be used to shift what is actually U.S.-source income to offshore tax-haven subsidiary corporations.

Along with income shifting and expatriation by corporations, tax havens in some cases apparently abet the outright evasion of taxes, in some cases by U.S. citizens. For example, income from illegal activity in the United States can be shielded from U.S. authorities if a tax haven offers sufficient bank secrecy. Or, taxes on legally generated U.S. income are apparently evaded in some cases by depositing the income in secrecy-protected foreign bank accounts.[40] The focus of this report, however, is the activities of multinational firms, so its concern with tax havens is more with legal (albeit what some might term "abusive") income shifting rather than outright tax evasion.

In part, the ability of firms to divert income from other foreign locations to tax havens has implications for the real location of investment: just because a tax haven is not the true source of income does not make the associated tax savings any less real for the underlying investment, wherever it may be located. We can interpret the effect of tax havens on actual investment in terms of the efficiency framework outlined in previous sections of the report. First, regarding the allocation of investment between the United States and foreign locations, existing data indicate that the United States is a relatively "high tax" country, even if tax havens are omitted from the calculation.[41] Thus, much of the income shifted to tax havens is likely shifted from countries whose taxes are lower than U.S. taxes to begin with. As a result, it is likely that tax havens on balance magnify the distorting effects of deferral, thus further diverting U.S. investment to foreign locations and, in turn, reducing economic efficiency and U.S. national welfare. This efficiency effect, however, may be mitigated by a reduction in the tax-induced distortion of location decisions across foreign countries.[42]

Along with efficiency effects, tax havens reduce tax revenue collections by capital-exporting countries. In the case of U.S. firms' use of tax havens, the revenue loss can accrue both to the United States (in the case of income shifted from domestic sources) and other countries (in the case of income shifted from other countries with higher taxes). Tax havens likewise have the potential of damaging perceptions of tax fairness when public reports appear of large firms and wealthy individuals using tax havens to avoid or evade substantial taxes.[43] Accordingly, a policy

---

[40] For a discussion of tax havens and illegal activities, see Martin A. Sullivan, "Sex, Drugs, and Tax Evasion," *Tax Notes*, June 18, 2007, pp. 1098-1100.

[41] 2002 Internal Revenue Service data on U.S.-controlled foreign subsidiaries show that subsidiaries pay, on average, a lower percentage of their pre-tax earnings in tax than do firms in the United States. This is true even for developed countries such as the United Kingdom and Canada.

[42] That tax havens actually stimulate investment in nearby higher-tax countries is argued in Mihir A. Desai, C. Fritz Foley, and James R. Hines, Jr., "Do Tax Havens Divert Economic Activity?" *Economics Letters*, vol. 90, 2006, pp. 219-224.

[43] Senate Finance Committee Chairman Max Baucus, for example, has observed that when tax havens are used for tax evasion "the honest American taxpayers who work hard, and do not have the ability to engage in offshore activity, are left holding the bill." Sen. Max Baucus, Hearing Statement Regarding Offshore Tax Evasion, May 3, 2007. Available as Finance Committee news release on the committee's website at

---

question is how tax evasion, or what might be termed "abusive" tax avoidance through tax havens, can be reduced.

One possible approach to tax havens is multilateral (that is, multi-country) action. The concept here is that tax havens flourish in part because of a lack of coordination in tax-administration between non-haven countries and that efforts to suppress tax-haven activities cannot be successful without solidarity among non-haven countries.[44] One prominent multilateral effort has been the Organization for Economic Cooperation and Development's (OECD's) "harmful tax practices project," initiated in 1996. The focus of the OECD's project has been to identify tax havens and to induce them to increase their "transparency" (presumably reduce secrecy about financial transactions) and to increase the number and scope of exchange of tax information agreements with tax havens.[45]

A unilateral approach was proposed by the Clinton Administration with its FY2001 budget proposal. The basis of the plan was to be a list of jurisdictions identified by the Treasury Department as tax havens. Foreign tax credits and the deferral benefit would be restricted for taxpayers using the identified tax havens.[46] More narrow unilateral approaches proposed in the past have primarily involved increasing information reporting requirements.

Several legislative proposals, including proposals in President Obama's budget, have been made to address evasion and avoidance. Some provisions were adopted in the Hire Act in 2010 (P.L. 111-147).[47]

General Reforms of the Corporate Tax and Implications for International Tax Treatment

Despite increasing globalization of the U.S. economy, foreign direct investment remains a small share of the U.S.-owned capital stock. For that reason, it would perhaps not be appropriate for international concerns to dominate the formulation of corporate tax policy. Nevertheless, there are specific forms of corporate tax revisions that might have important consequences for international taxation.

---

[44] To illustrate, imagine a situation where country A has exchange of information agreements both with country B and tax haven H. Country B, however, has no exchange agreement with the tax haven. Conceivably, would-be taxpayers from country A could channel tax-saving tax haven transactions through country B.

[45] Jeffrey Owens, Director, OECD Centre for Tax Policy and Administration, "OECD's Work in Counteracting the Use of Tax Havens to Evade Taxes," unpublished paper presented at the American Enterprise Institute, December 11, 2006. Some U.S. critics of the OECD criticized what they saw as the initiative's underlying premise that low taxes are suspect. It was indeed partly on this basis that the Bush administration persuaded the OECD to focus on transparency and exchange of information rather than efforts to persuade targeted countries to change their tax practices towards non-residents. See Hon. Paul O'Neill, Secretary of the Treasury, testimony before the Senate Committee on Governmental Affairs, Permanent Subcommittee on Investigations, July 18, 2001. Available at the committee's website, at http://hsgac.senate.gov/071801_psioneil.htm.

[46] For a description of the proposal, see U.S. Congress, Joint Committee on Taxation, *Description of Revenue Proposals Contained in the President's Fiscal Year 2001 Budget Proposals* (Washington: GPO, 2000), pp. 500-509.

[47] See CRS Report R40623, *Tax Havens: International Tax Avoidance and Evasion*, by Jane G. Gravelle for descriptions.

Under the current U.S. system, taxes on corporate profits at the individual level (dividends and capital gains) tend to be collected (due to tax treaties) on a residence basis. If taxes at the individual level could be increased and taxes at the corporate level decreased, the tax would shift towards a residence-based system without any other changes and without any additional concerns about portfolio substitution. In 2003, relief for double taxation was provided by reducing the tax rate on corporate dividends from the ordinary tax rate to 15% for those in brackets above the 15% rate, and to 5% for others. The 5% rate is now scheduled to fall to zero.

Using 2004 figures, where data on qualified dividends are available, the 35% corporate tax rate could have been rolled back to a 31% rate, or even less, for the same revenue cost if a corporate rate reduction rather than reductions in the individual level tax had occurred.[48] There are many other potential changes that could raise revenue to permit a further lowering of the corporate rate. At the individual level, these might include higher capital gains tax rates, accrual taxation of gains on corporate stock, and limits or modest taxes on retirement savings (which would benefit from corporate rate reductions). At the corporate level, a number of base broadening provisions might be considered. It could be feasible to lower the corporate tax rate to 25% with relatively modest changes in tax rules.[49]

A lower U.S. corporate tax is desirable if one believes that the most serious distortion in the international tax system is the tendency of capital to flow to low-tax foreign jurisdictions because of deferral. Such a proposition is a reasonable one, as the United States is generally a high-tax country. Lower corporate tax rates are also responsive to concerns that portfolio substitution disfavors U.S. owned firms. Nevertheless, even significant reductions in the U.S. tax rate are unlikely to have significant effects on overall U.S. output because the corporate tax is relatively small compared to GDP. A recent estimate suggests that lowering the rate to 25% without making any other changes would increase U.S. output by only 2/10 of 1% of GDP.[50]

---

[48] In 2004, taxable qualified dividends for individual income taxes were $104 billion according to the Statistics of Income data. Assuming a 15% rate differential, rolling back the provision for dividends would have raised revenues by $15.6 billion. The gain from raising the capital gains tax rate back to 20% depends on the behavioral response—how much individuals reduce their realizations, given tax increases. Based on the realization responses the Joint Tax Committee used in the past, and the Congressional Budget Office baseline, the gain for capital gains would be $9.2 billion. If the realizations response were based on the response used by the Congressional Budget Office in projecting the baseline, it would raise $12.7 billion. There is some evidence that even that response is too large as discussed in CRS Report R41364, *Capital Gains Tax Options: Behavioral Responses and Revenues*, by Jane G. Gravelle If the revenue gain is to be used to reduce the corporate tax and raise after-tax profits, they need to be grossed up by (1-t) where t is the effective individual tax rate on an additional dollar of corporate after-tax profits. The estimate assumes an average tax rate of 25% and that half of the income goes to non-taxable recipients such as pension funds, for an overall rate of 12.5%. Corporate tax revenues were $189 billion in FY2004, but this value was unusually low because of bonus depreciation. Adjusting for bonus depreciation brings the revenue to $236 billion. (For a discussion, see CRS Report RL33672, *Revenue Feedback from the 2001-2004 Tax Cuts*, by Jane G. Gravelle.) The revenue gains divided by the gross-up factor and then by corporate tax receipts indicate the percentage reduction in the corporate tax (12% and 13.5% respectively), which are then multiplied by the 35% rate to determine the percentage point reduction.

[49] Taxing capital gains at full rates would have raised, for 2004, $7 billion to $20 billion, or even more, allowing a rate decrease of one to three percentage points. Accrual taxation would yield dramatically larger revenues. Two examples of corporate base broadeners include the production activities deduction for domestic manufacturing and certain industries, and the title passage rule, which is a rule allowing an arbitrary allocation of income from U.S. exports to be assigned to foreign-source income for purposes of the foreign tax credit limit (effectively an export subsidy). According to tax expenditure estimates, the production activities deduction (which is being phased in) will reach a cost of $10 billion by FY2010. The title passage rule costs about $6 billion. These two corporate provisions should permit a three percentage point reduction, bringing the rate to between 27% and 28%.

[50] CRS Report R41743, *International Corporate Tax Rate Comparisons and Policy Implications*, by Jane G. Gravelle.

While international concerns should not necessarily dominate the issues surrounding corporate tax policy,[51] they do suggest the economic desirability of certain types of corporate tax reforms that would improve economic efficiency in the international area.

Author Contact Information

Jane G. Gravelle
Senior Specialist in Economic Policy
jgravelle@crs.loc.gov, 7-7829

Acknowledgments

This report was originally written with David Brumbaugh.

---

[51] Two reasons to provide relief at the individual level are (1) to focus tax cuts on marginal investment, which is more likely to be taxable investment to individuals rather than investment in pension funds and retirement accounts; and (2) to reduce the distortion that capital gains taxes impose on the willingness to realize gains and adjust assets. This latter distortion, however, would be improved if an accrual basis capital gains tax on corporate stock were adopted. Such a move would also raise a great deal of revenue that could be used to lower corporate tax rates. Doing so would also end concerns about using corporations with lower tax rates to shelter income.